CALLING
AND
WORK

THEOLOGY OF WORK PROJECT

CALLING
AND
WORK

THE BIBLE AND YOUR WORK
Study Series

HENDRICKSON
PUBLISHERS

Theology of Work
The Bible and Your Work Study Series: Calling and Work

© 2015 by Hendrickson Publishers Marketing, LLC
P.O. Box 3473
Peabody, Massachusetts 01961-3473

ISBN 978-1-61970-693-4

Adapted from the *Theology of Work Bible Commentary*, copyright © 2014 by the Theology of Work Project, Inc. All rights reserved.

William Messenger, Executive Editor, Theology of Work Project
Sean McDonough, Biblical Editor, Theology of Work Project
Patricia Anders, Editorial Director, Hendrickson Publishers

Contributors:

Christopher Gilbert, "Calling and Work" Bible Study
William Messenger, "Calling and Work" in the *Theology of Work Bible Commentary*

The Theology of Work Project is an independent, international organization dedicated to researching, writing, and distributing materials with a biblical perspective on work. The Project's primary mission is to produce resources covering every book of the Bible plus major topics in today's workplaces. Wherever possible, the Project collaborates with other faith-and-work organizations, churches, universities and seminaries to help equip people for meaningful, productive work of every kind.

Printed in the United States of America

First Printing—November 2015

Contents

The Theology of Work

Work is not only a human calling, but also a divine one. "In the beginning God created the heavens and the earth." God worked to create us and created us to work. "The LORD God took the man and put him in the garden of Eden to till it and keep it" (Gen. 2:15). God also created work to be good, even if it's hard to see in a fallen world. To this day, God calls us to work to support ourselves and to serve others (Eph. 4:28).

Work can accomplish many of God's purposes for our lives—the basic necessities of food and shelter, as well as a sense of fulfillment and joy. Our work can create ways to help people thrive; it can discover the depths of God's creation; and it can bring us into wonderful relationships with co-workers and those who benefit from our work (customers, clients, patients, and so forth).

Yet many people face drudgery, boredom, or exploitation at work. We have bad bosses, hostile relationships, and unfriendly work environments. Our work seems useless, unappreciated, faulty, frustrating. We don't get paid enough. We get stuck in dead-end jobs or laid off or fired. We fail. Our skills become obsolete. It's a struggle just to make ends meet. But how can this be if God created work to be good—and what can we do about it? God's answers for these questions must be somewhere in the Bible, but where?

The Theology of Work Project's mission has been to study what the Bible says about work and to develop resources to apply the

Christian faith to our work. It turns out that every book of the Bible gives practical, relevant guidance that can help us do our jobs better, improve our relationships at work, support ourselves, serve others more effectively, and find meaning and value in our work. The Bible shows us how to live all of life—including work—in Christ. Only in Jesus can we and our work be transformed to become the blessing it was always meant to be.

To put it another way, if we are not following Christ during the 100,000 hours of our lives that we spend at work, are we really following Christ? Our lives are more than just one day a week at church. The fact is that God cares about our life *every day of the week*. But how do we become equipped to follow Jesus at work? In the same ways we become equipped for every aspect of life in Christ—listening to sermons, modeling our lives on others' examples, praying for God's guidance, and most of all by studying the Bible and putting it into practice.

This Theology of Work series contains a variety of books to help you apply the Scriptures and Christian faith to your work. This Bible study is one volume in the series The Bible and Your Work. It is intended for those who want to explore what the Bible says about work and how to apply it to their work in positive, practical ways. Although it can be used for individual study, Bible study is especially effective with a group of people committed to practicing what they read in Scripture. In this way, we gain from one another's perspectives and are encouraged to actually *do* what we read in Scripture. Because of the direct focus on work, The Bible and Your Work studies are especially suited for Bible studies *at* work or *with* other people in similar occupations. The following lessons are designed for thirty-minute lunch breaks (or perhaps breakfast before work) during a five-day work week.

Christians today recognize God's calling to us in and through our work—for ourselves and for those whom we serve. May God use this book to help you follow Christ in every sphere of life and work.

Will Messenger, Executive Editor
Theology of Work Project

Introduction to Calling and Work

An Explanation of the Study

Work is a fact of life for everyone. Whether we get paid for our work at not, we all engage in activity intended to produce useful results. This is work. Most of us will *need* to work in order to support ourselves and other people who depend on us. So, at some point in our lives, most of us begin to ask what kind of work we want to do as an occupation. In fact, we may face this question many times over the course of our lives. For some of us, we have an apparently easy answer: From early years, we just know we are made to fly planes, teach middle school, or become a graphic artist—and we have the resources available to attain to this.

But some of us can spend years working without much of a sense of vocation. For others of us, circumstances—such as family needs and expectations, political oppression and war, or accident or illness—can limit our freedom to choose our work. Insufficient money, educational opportunity, or social resources can be limiting factors for us as well. Or it may be that what we *want* to do just cannot meet our needs.

It is in this context that we ask what the Bible says about the question, "Is God calling me to a particular job, profession, or type of work?" This question matters because God is interested in our work. In the Bible we see God calling some people to particular work, and we find God's guidance for everyone's work. We will explore biblical accounts of God's calling and work-related guidance in depth. In these stories, we might not always see the word *call* used to describe God's guidance to jobs, occupations, or tasks, but these occurrences do correspond to what we usually mean by an occupational "calling."

So we can say yes, God does lead people to particular types of employment. But in the Bible, the concept of calling goes deeper than our work. God calls us into unity with himself in *every* aspect of life. Jesus makes a very personal plea in his call of "Follow me!" The calling to follow Christ lies at the root of every other calling and is not limited to becoming a professional church worker. People in *every* walk of life are called to follow Christ with equal depth and commitment, both on the job and off.

Chapter 1

God's Call—What Do We Mean?

Lesson #1: Call to Belong to Christ and Participate in His Redemptive Work in the World (2 Corinthians 5:15–6:2)

The calling to belong to Christ goes deeper than the kind of work-place "calling" that is the main focus of this Bible study. For this reason, it is important to start our exploration of "calling" with the call to follow Jesus. But what do we mean by "calling"?

The biblical use of the word *call* most often refers to the way that God draws people to himself in Christ, participating in his redemptive work in the world. The Apostle Paul, in particular, understands God's calling in this, whether or not he uses the word *call*. In Romans 1:6 he says, "Including yourselves who are called to belong to Jesus Christ." Here, we have the sense of a calling to belong to the family of God. Then in Romans 8:28, he describes calling as participating with God's purposes: "All things work together for good for those who love God, who are called according to his purpose." And in 2 Corinthians 5:17–20, he elaborates that God's purpose is the redemption (or "reconciliation") of the world:

> So if anyone is in Christ, there is a new creation: everything old has passed away; see, everything has become new! All this is from God, who reconciled us to himself through Christ, and has given us the ministry of reconciliation; that is, in Christ God was reconciling the world to himself, not counting their trespasses against them, and entrusting the message of reconciliation to us.

> So we are ambassadors for Christ, since God is making his appeal through us; we entreat you on behalf of Christ, be reconciled to God.

The call to redemption is open to everyone.

So we understand here that this is a call to a restored relationship with God, with other people, and with the world we inhabit. It encompasses every aspect of who we are and all that we do. It reminds us that the call to a *particular* kind of work is subsumed in the call to belong to Christ and to participate in his redemption of the world.

 Food for Thought

Watch the discussion with Haddon Robinson, Alice Mathews, and Mart DeHaan on the meaning of "call" at www.theologyofwork .org/resources/understanding-gods-call-on-our-lives. What ideas spring to mind when you hear the words, "God called me to . . ."? Why do you think a call from God has been limited to mean working in church ministry or mission? What if it is meant to be much broader than that?

_____

_____

_____

_____

_____

_____

_____

If we understand that a call from God is all encompassing, then whatever work we do is an integral part of our participation in the life of Christ himself. His work of creation underlies the act of creativity and production in the universe, for "all things came into being through him, and without him not one thing came into being" (John 1:3). His work of redemption can occur in every workplace through justice, healing, reconciliation, compassion, kindness, humility, and patience (Col. 3:12).

Our work as Christ's people also integrates both creation and redemption. It continues the work of creation, production, and sustenance that God delegated to humanity in the Garden of Eden. It embodies the work of reconciliation and redemption that Jesus modeled in his life and fulfilled on the cross. The Bible does not say that the work of redemption has superseded the work of creation. Both continue, and we can take it as a general rule that as Christians we are commanded to participate in both the work of creation and redemption.

 Food for Thought

Do you think of your work as primarily creative (e.g., designing, making, and creating) or redemptive (e.g., healing, restoring, or fixing)? How might the integration of redemption and creation in the work of Christ impact the way you do the work you are doing now?

_____

_____

_____

_____

_____

_____

Prayer

Pause for a few moments of silence to reflect on this lesson. Then offer a prayer, either spontaneous or by using the following:

> *Lord,*
>
> *Open our hearts to the fullness of who you are and the amazing breadth of the purposes for which you call us. We want to be found as stewards of your creation and as agents of your reconciliation. Help us to understand what this means wherever we are today.*
>
> *Amen.*

Lesson #2: The Universal Call to Work (Genesis 1:26–30; 2:4–15)

Before we can discuss the possibility of God's guidance to a particular kind of work, we must recognize that God intends for everyone to do work of some kind, to the degree they are able. God *created* people to work and he *commands* people to work (Gen. 1:27–28) according to their ability. (For a deeper study of this truth, see *Genesis 1–12* in The Bible and Your Work Study Series by the Theology of Work Project.)

At the beginning of the Bible, God builds work into the very essence of being human. He creates people in his own image, and as the Creator, he himself is a worker. From the book of Genesis when God put Adam in the garden for the purpose of working it, to various other similar stories throughout Scripture to the book of Revelation, work is a given in all the ages of human history. There is work in the Garden of Eden, and there is work in the new heaven and the new earth.

Food for Thought

Read the following Scripture texts: Genesis 1:27–28; 2:15, 19–20; Exodus 20:9; Isaiah 65:21–22; 2 Thessalonians 3:10; and Revelation 21:24–26. To what extent are these commands, and how do they reveal our purpose as human beings?

_____

_____

_____

_____

_____

_____

_____

Based on these passages, we could say that *everyone* is called to work, as long as we recognize that in this sense "called" really means "created" and "commanded" to work.

God created you as a worker, and he commands you to work, even if he doesn't send you a specific job offer. It can be difficult to discern the particular work God may be calling you to, but there can be no doubt that he made you as a worker and that he expects you to work to the degree you are able.

It is becoming clearer to historians that as Christians took this mandate seriously from the earliest times, the world has been uniquely blessed economically and socially. Vishal Mangalwadi, for example, devotes a chapter in *The Book that Made Your World* to the Christian influence on work and the development of technologies that set the Western world apart until the present day.

 *Food for Thought*

If God created people to work, then why do we so often regard or experience work as something to be avoided?

_____

_____

_____

_____

_____

_____

_____

Prayer

Pause for a few moments of silence to reflect on this lesson. Then offer a prayer, either spontaneous or by using the following:

Lord,

Guide us to fulfill your call for us to work in accordance with your purposes. For those of us who have the work we need, give us grace to trust you in our work. For those of us needing employment, open pathways to work to which we can apply ourselves faithfully. For those of us who can create employment opportunities for others, guide our endeavors to become avenues of service, justice, and faithfulness.

Amen.

Chapter 2
God's Calling—The Big Picture

Lesson #1: Calling to Life, Not Only to Work
(Colossians 3:12–17; 4:5–6)

Workaholism may not be a clinical diagnosis, but the term is coined for a human condition many of us have experienced in one way or another. It can occur when we allow work to dominate our lives or become our primary source of meaning, or when financial circumstances are so difficult that it appears the only solution is to work longer and harder. It plays out when we devote ourselves to the issues of our workplace at the expense of other responsibilities, such as friendship, marriage, and parenthood.

But work is only one aspect of our lives. God created us to be multifaceted, allowing us to reflect his glory in many different ways. Before exploring God's call to work in greater depth, let's pause a moment to make sure we understand the proper role of work in life.

 Food for Thought

Consider Colossians 3:17: "Whatever you do, in word or deed, do everything in the name of the Lord Jesus." What are some things that are part of "everything" that go beyond your daily work? In order to honor Christ as your Lord, what is required in these areas of your life?

_____

_____

———————————————————————————

———————————————————————————

———————————————————————————

———————————————————————————

———————————————————————————

———————————————————————————

First, it is vital to realize that our jobs are not necessarily the most significant aspect of our calling or our service in Christ's broad work of redemption. We serve Christ in many ways besides working a job that earns a paycheck.

For one thing, not all work is paid work. In fact, God's primary work for us may be unpaid work, such as raising children, caring for a disabled or elderly family member, or tutoring students after school. And even if we have paid work, God seldom calls us into jobs that completely prevent us from also serving others through unpaid work.

So it is possible that the most critical work God calls you to may be outside your job. Your job may meet your need for money—which in itself fulfills part of God's command to work—but it may not fulfill all the other purposes God has for your work. Conversely, those doing unpaid work, such as caring for children and for aged or incapacitated people, may also have another, paid job. Whether or not the work we do is paid has little to do with how important it is in God's eyes.

Also, what others might regard as a hobby might be for you the most meaningful work God has for you. You might work at writing, painting, music, acting, astronomy, leading a youth group, volunteering at a historical society, maintaining a nature reserve, or a thousand other kinds of work. If something like this is your calling, then you will probably take it quite seriously while still earning your living in another way.

There is a distinction between work and leisure, although it is quite blurry at times. Work is done in order to accomplish something beyond the enjoyment of the activity itself. Leisure is done for its own sake. But any given activity could be work—paid or unpaid—in some cases and leisure in others. Perhaps the ideal situation is that our needs are met by work we enjoy doing for its own sake: "I can't believe I get paid to do this!" But nothing in Scripture suggests that we should expect this as a matter of course.

 Food for Thought

Consider the choices you have made in regard to paid or unpaid work. What was the real attraction to the task? What is the reward you seek from it? Or was it the enjoyment of the task itself—or a bit of both? How well can you discern a sense of God's call in the kind of attraction and the sense of reward your work offers you?

_____

_____

_____

_____

_____

_____

_____

_____

Second, we must take care not to let work dominate the other facets of our lives. Even if God leads us to a particular job, we need to set limits to that work to make room for the other dimensions of God's call in our lives.

For example, if God leads you to be married *and* to be a small business owner, then you will have to balance the time and responsibilities of both callings. At times, you may have to cancel plans with your spouse to handle a business situation. But you may also have to hire additional help—even at the expense of some profitability—to prevent yourself from effectively abandoning your spouse. Likewise, if you feel a call to volunteer work and you also have children to parent, then your children will have to recognize that sometimes you may be off serving others. Yet you need to prioritize the needs of your children above volunteer activity, no matter how worthy the task.

If you are unemployed and seeking work while caring for a disabled spouse or child, it may be difficult to know whether to turn down work because it would interfere with your care duties, or to alter your care routines to accommodate the work needed to support your family. It is comforting to realize, however, that God knows the full range of your needs even before you ask. The help of friends and your Christian community can be essential in helping you decide and follow God's guidance.

Work should not crowd out leisure, rest, and worship. (For a fuller treatment of work and rest, see *Exodus* in this Theology of Work Project Bible study series.) Although there is no formula for balancing work and other elements of life, it is crucial not to let a sense of calling to a job prevent us from recognizing God's calling in those other areas.

 *Food for Thought*

What are your biggest traps for losing your balance between work and other facets of your life? What might be some strategies you could implement to integrate the various aspects of everyday life and work?

_____

_____

_____

_____

_____

_____

_____

_____

Prayer

Pause for a few moments of silence to reflect on this lesson. Then offer a prayer, either spontaneous or by using the following:

Lord,

How easily our lives become fractured when we are faced with attractive, loud, or urgent calls on our time and talents. Help us to become more aware of your priorities for our lives and learn to hear your voice when our duties or opportunities seem to conflict. Grant us your encouragement and grace in the midst of what may feel too hard for us.

Amen.

Lesson #2: God's Guidance to Particular Work (Exodus 31:1–11; Philippians 4:4–9, 12–13)

Now that we have been careful to keep in view the broadest sense of God's call on our lives, we are ready to delve into the possibility of knowing God's guidance to a particular type of work. So far, we have discussed that:

1. Everyone is called to belong to Christ, participating in his creative and redemptive work;

2. everyone is commanded to work to the degree we are able; and

3. God calls us to a whole life, not just to a job.

Putting these together leads us to conclude that our profession is not by itself God's highest concern for us. God is much more concerned that you come under the saving grace of Christ and participate in his work of creation and redemption. He calls you to do your work—whatever it is—in accordance with his word. Exactly what kind of work you do is probably a lower-level concern to God.

 Food for Thought:

How do you respond to the idea that your particular job may not be the most important thing God cares about for you? If the job is not so critical, then what is the important issue for God?

_____

_____

_____

_____

_____

_____

_____

_____

Even though it might feel crucial to us get the best job or career we can, the exact kind of work we do *is* a lower-level concern of God's. But just because getting us into the right job or career is not God's highest concern, it doesn't mean that it is of *no* concern. We know it does concern him because the distinctive work of the Holy Spirit throughout Scripture guides and empowers people for the life and work to which God leads them.

> To each is given the manifestation of the Spirit for the common good. To one is given through the Spirit the utterance of wisdom, and to another the utterance of knowledge according to the same Spirit, to another faith by the same Spirit, to another gifts of healing by the one Spirit, to another the working of miracles, to another prophecy, to another the discernment of spirits, to another various kinds of tongues, to another the interpretation of tongues. All these are activated by one and the same Spirit, who allots to each one individually just as the Spirit chooses. (1 Cor. 12:7–11)

In the Old Testament, we see God calling people to particular jobs and giving them the needed skills, as for example with Bezalel and Oholiab in the building of the tabernacle (Exod. 31:1–11). Or with Ruth, who took on the backbreaking work of gleaning, when God equipped her with grace and humility in her quest to get her mother-in-law Naomi's inheritance restored. Or with David, whom God equipped with the wisdom and judgment to be a king/military leader, and the creative ability of a singer/songwriter.

In the time since Christ, the Spirit routinely guides believers to particular work, giving us the skills we need to do that work (1 Cor. 12:7–10). Not only does he provide guidance in *what kind* of work we do, but he also provides guidance in *how* to do that work.

 *Food for Thought*

When it comes to a particular task, we often have the attitude of either "I can" or "I can't." But Paul writes, "I can do all things through him who strengthens me" (see Phil. 4:12–13). Do you feel God has equipped you for your work? If not, why? How can you apply that understanding to your work, if you don't already? How can you remind yourself of this throughout the day?

_____

_____

_____

_____

_____

_____

_____

Prayer

Pause for a few moments of silence to reflect on this lesson. Then offer a prayer, either spontaneous or by using the following:

Lord,

As followers of Christ, we know that you care for our whole lives above all. Within this, you have a concern for the particular work we do, so we ask that you guide us into a clearer understanding of our vocations and how you want us to do that work.

Amen.

Lesson #3: A Direct, Unmistakable Call to Particular Work (Exodus 3:1–12; Mark 3:13–19; Acts 13:1–3)

The call to follow Jesus is certainly the ultimate call on our lives. With that understanding, let us explore in Scripture the particular calls to work God bestows on his people.

On occasion, God simply tells people what he wants them to do. Throughout the sixty-six books, we discover a hundred or so people called by God in this sense. God called Noah to build the ark (Gen. 6:14–22). He called Moses and Aaron to liberate Israel from Egypt (Exod. 3:4; 28:1). He called Abraham and Sarah to move to a foreign land and herd sheep and cattle there, in a land destined to become the homeland for their offspring. He called prophets—such as Samuel (1 Sam. 3:10), Jeremiah (Jer. 1:4–5), Amos (Amos 7:15), Isaiah (Isa. 6:1–6)—to reform the religious and civic aspects of Israelite society. He placed people in political leadership, including Joseph, Daniel, Gideon, Saul, and David. Jesus called the apostles and some other of his disciples (e.g., Mark 3:13–19), and the Holy Spirit called Barnabas and Saul to be missionaries (Acts 13:2). Although the word *call* is not always used, the unmistakable direction of God for a particular person to do a particular job is clear in these cases.

 Food for Thought

How clear is God's call in your own life? Has God unmistakably called you to the work you are doing? Would you regard it as a direct call in the way described in this lesson?

_____

_____

_____

_____

Aside from these examples, few people in the Bible received a direct call from God to a particular kind of work. This strongly suggests that a direct calling from God is also rare today.

If God is clearly calling you to particular work, then you probably don't need guidance from a study such as this, except perhaps for affirmation that this type of calling does occur in the Bible, although relatively infrequently. (The extent of this infrequency becomes more apparent when we consider the vast time periods in the biblical record of Israel where no one with a particular call is recorded.) Therefore, we will not discuss direct, unmistakable, personal calling further. We will instead focus on whether God leads us to particular types of work through more ordinary and perhaps more subtle means, such as our study of Scripture, the requests we make in prayer, the wisdom of our Christian community, and the insights we may gain through reflection.

Although it is beyond the scope of this study to consider how we develop a general attentiveness to God's guidance in our lives, in the next chapter we will look at three major considerations for discerning God's *vocational* guidance.

 Food for Thought

When someone speaks to you of a clear call from God in his or her life, how do you respond? Are you skeptical? What do you look for in such a claim in order to give it credence?

Prayer

Pause for a few moments of silence to reflect on this lesson. Then offer a prayer, either spontaneous or by using the following:

Lord,

However your calling comes to us, we would like to be clear in regard to the work you are leading us to do. Please help us to get beyond our fears and self-interests, to trust you, and to be willing to hear and follow your call, however you deliver it.

Amen.

Chapter 3

Discerning God's Guidance to a Particular Kind of Work

Lesson #1: Guidance to a Job or Profession—The Needs of the World (Matthew 25:31–46)

Perhaps the single strongest indicator of what God wants us to do is to see how we fit into what needs to be done to make the world more as God intends it to be. We have a good sense from Scripture of what God wants the world to be like: full of justice, opportunity, beauty, and truth, a place where humanity and nature are in harmony, where the needs of all people are met, and there is freedom from disease, injury, oppression, abuse, and deception. Since the world is not like this at present, a good way to begin hearing a call is to commit ourselves to doing whatever we can do to make the world more as God wants it to be.

You may immediately jump to immense global problems, but that's not necessarily God's immediate concern for us. More simply, we should be occupied with doing anything that must be done to meet real needs, which could be as basic as earning a living to support yourself and your family.

The Needs of the World Begin at Home

To the degree that we are able, God calls us to meet our own needs and the needs of our immediate families. Consider the following:

The good leave an inheritance to their children's children. (Prov. 13:22)

The wise woman builds her house, but the foolish tears it down with her own hands. (Prov. 14:1)

Whoever does not provide for relatives, and especially for family members, has denied the faith and is worse than an unbeliever. (1 Tim. 5:8)

Let people learn to devote themselves to good works in order to meet urgent needs, so that they may not be unproductive. (Titus 3:14)

 Food for Thought

Do these verses in any way change your view of working to provide for your family? If so, how? If not, why?

_____

_____

_____

_____

_____

_____

The Needs of the World Include Our Neighbors

God also calls us to help meet the needs of our neighbors and communities:

Happy are those who are kind to the poor. (Prov. 14:21)

Aspire to live quietly, to mind your own affairs, and to work with your hands, as we directed you. (1 Thess. 4:11)

The crowds asked [John the Baptist], "What then should we do?" In reply he said to them, "Whoever has two coats must share with anyone who has none; and whoever has food must do likewise." (Luke 3:10–11)

A generous person will be enriched, and one who gives water will get water. (Prov. 11:25)

Then the king will say to those at his right hand, "Come, you that are blessed by my Father, inherit the kingdom prepared for you from the foundation of the world; for I was hungry and you gave me food, I was thirsty and you gave me something to drink, I was a stranger and you welcomed me, I was naked and you gave me clothing, I was sick and you took care of me, I was in prison and you visited me." (Matt. 25:34–36)

 Food for Thought

It seems that there will always be someone who needs our help. When our family is cared for, then there will be others to care for. What are the needs in your neighborhood that you see and can respond to?

_____

_____

_____

_____

_____

_____

_____

The Needs of the World Include the World beyond Our Neighborhoods

Working to serve the good of the larger society is also a biblical imperative.

> Build houses and live in them; plant gardens and eat what they produce. Take wives and have sons and daughters; take wives for your sons, and give your daughters in marriage, that they may bear sons and daughters; multiply there, and do not decrease. But seek the welfare of the city where I have sent you into exile, and pray to the LORD on its behalf, for in its welfare you will find your welfare. (Jer. 29:5–7)

Modern communication systems make us aware that the world is broken in ways that only global responses can meet. We see in the daily news when goods, services, and workers are needed on the other side of the globe, and it may be that we are in a position to meet those needs. Other times, it is not a matter of sending aid somewhere else, but of cooperating on a global scale to solve problems affecting the whole world. The more we know, or can learn, about these needs and the more ability we have to help meet them, the stronger the biblical imperative to work on them. A herder struggling to support a family in a less developed county might not have much of a calling to help eradicate malaria, polio, or cancer. But a biologist, public health worker, or a potential wealthy donor might.

The way we direct the fruit of our labor to help others is as narrow as our own homes and as broad as the planet. Human need that we allow ourselves to feel in our own hearts definitely prompts the most creative and purposeful thought and response. And when this happens, we usually have some clarity that we are responding to a genuine call from God.

For example, rather than moving away to find work elsewhere, you might be in a good position to run for elected office in your current city or town. On the other hand, you might be one of the few people willing to document human rights abuses in a country half-way around the world. Or you might become convinced that teaching troubled youth is more pressing.

Conversely, it might become clear that something in your life other than your job or career is the most important way you are helping to meet the world's needs. If you have children, then the work of raising them certainly comes to mind. It would be pointless to get a job counseling troubled youth, for example, only to neglect your own children. Or, if your work brings you wealth, you might find that giving or investing to meet other's needs is as significant as, or more important than, the goods or services produced by your work itself.

The point is that God gives everyone the ability to recognize something of what the world needs, near or far, large or small, immediate or long term. He seems to expect us to notice it and to get to work, rather than wait for a special call from him.

 Food for Thought

To what extent do you think you are open to the needs of the world as described in this lesson? Are there any blind spots you need to address? Where is your heart most drawn—to your home, your neighborhood, or somewhere beyond?

_____

_____

_____

_____

_____

_____

_____

_____

Prayer

Pause for a few moments of silence to reflect on this lesson. Then offer a prayer, either spontaneous or by using the following:

Lord,

How often we can miss the obvious. Please help us to open our hearts to the needs close to us, as well as those far away. Help us to find joy in the obedience of working to meet those needs with whatever resource, gift, and ability you have provided to us.

Amen.

Lesson #2: Guidance to a Job or Profession—Your Skills and Gifts (1 Corinthians 12:4–27)

As we began to see in a previous lesson (Exod. 31:1–11), the skills and gifts we receive from God are also a means of guidance to the work God calls us to do. Throughout the Bible, we find descriptions of the wide variety of gifts and skills that God imparts:

Do those who plow for sowing plow continually? Do they continually open and harrow their ground? When they have leveled its surface, do they not scatter dill, sow cummin, and plant wheat in rows and barley in its proper place, and spelt as the border? For they are well instructed; their God teaches them. (Isa. 28:24–26)

> We have gifts that differ according to the grace given to us:
> prophecy, in proportion to faith; ministry, in ministering; the
> teacher, in teaching; the exhorter, in exhortation; the giver, in
> generosity; the leader, in diligence; the compassionate, in cheer-
> fulness. (Rom. 12:6–8)

As the passage from Romans suggests, Paul's discussion of God's gifts is usually in the context of use in the church (see especially 1 Cor. 12:7–10). But if all work done by Christians is done for the Lord (Col. 3:23), then God's gifts are also given for use in every kind of workplace. Indeed, most workplaces need the same giftedness as churches: prophetic people who can discern the truth and see what is truly valuable; ministers (another word for administrators) who can organize and manage systems and workforces; teachers who can impart expertise to those who need it; exhorters who help workers develop character and resilience; colleagues who are generous with their time, expertise, networks, and encouragement; leaders who can communicate a vision and inspire groups to attain it; servers and agents who truly care about customers, co-workers, and their community; people who radiate the joy of God's presence in every walk of life.

Every workplace needs the whole variety of gifts and skills that God imparts to his people. Therefore, your particular gifts and skills provide an element of guidance in discerning God's particular calling for your work.

 Food for Thought

In Isaiah 28, the prophet suggests that growing crops is a calling because God imparts the skills that farmers need to accomplish this task. Does the same apply to all occupations? In what ways does God give you and the people in your current occupation the ability to recognize the best ways to do your work and the skills to carry it out?

_____

_____

_____

_____

_____

_____

_____

_____

Gift-Assessment Tools

A number of tools have been developed to help people discern their gifts and make use of them in workplace settings. However, there is a danger in paying *too* much attention to our skills and gifts. The present generation of urban Westerners is the most gift-analyzed in human history, yet it seems that we are also experiencing a growing self-absorption, crowding out attention to the needs of the world.

The passages above say that God gives gifts for the common good, not just personal satisfaction. And God often gives people his gifts *after* they begin the work to which he calls them. Paying too much attention to the gifts you already have can keep you from receiving new gifts that God may want to give you.

Nonetheless, the gifts you already have may give you some indication about how to best meet the needs of the world. If you are gifted and trained in music, and if your musical talent is needed somewhere in the world, then it may be less likely that God is calling you to a career in cancer research, compared to someone who has a degree in biochemistry. But this is not absolute. God works in mysterious ways! Career guidance via skills and gifts is a difficult balancing act, which is why the best advice is to seek counsel from your relationship with God and fellow Christians.

Here again, we must not become focused on work to the exclusion of the rest of life. God also gives us gifts for our family life, friendships, recreation, volunteering, and the whole breadth of life's activities. God does not intend for us to become obsessed with finding the perfect match for our gifts.

 Food for Thought

Have you had the opportunity to use a gift-assessment tool? If so, what value has it added to your career/job? What have been the limitations of that experience? How else have you become aware of your skills and gifts?

_____

_____

_____

_____

_____

_____

_____

Prayer

Pause for a few moments of silence to reflect on this lesson. Then offer a prayer, either spontaneous or by using the following:

Lord,

We recognize that hearing your call to particular work is fraught with our tendency to reduce life to our own interests. As we consider who we are called to be today, please provide the wisdom and counsel of good people to take us past our blind spots.

Amen.

Lesson #3: Guidance to a Job or Profession—Your Truest Desires (Psalm 21:1–7; 145:15–21)

A common fear that can affect new Christians and delay the maturity of older Christians is the expectation that if God calls them to some task, it will be something really hard, something they never would have chosen to do. We seem to expect that if God calls us to a particular job, then it will be something we hate. Otherwise, why would God have to call us to do it? A common mistake is to think that God's highest call is to make you a missionary to a country you don't want to go to. Actually, the best missionaries tend to have a great attraction to the people, place, and culture where is God calling them.

And in any case, being a missionary is no higher calling than any other. God is the source of *every* skill, and he calls people into *every* kind of work that makes the world more as he wants it to be. If God is guiding you toward a particular job or profession, then it's more likely you will find it satisfies your deepest heartfelt desires. You just have to get in touch with what those are!

Food for Thought

Is there something you fear God would call you to, something you absolutely don't want to be part of? What if that fear is blinding you to his real calling to a kind of work that fits you perfectly? What abilities has God given you for the work you have now?

_____

_____

_____

_____

_____

_____

_____

_____

The Bible says that your deepest desires are important to God:

> Take delight in the LORD, and he will give you the desires of your heart. (Ps. 37:4)

> He fulfills the desire of all who fear him; he also hears their cry, and saves them. (Ps. 145:19)

> "Blessed are those who hunger and thirst for righteousness, for they will be filled." (Matt. 5:6)

> "Until now you have not asked for anything in my name. Ask and you will receive, so that your joy may be complete." (John 16:24)

Clark, a community development worker, was so engaged with juvenile offenders in the criminal justice system that after almost a decade he broke down with Chronic Fatigue Syndrome. Clark's job was to lead a team in designing and implementing programs to move released offenders into jobs. While immersed in this task, he was sure he was living out his highest aspirations as a Christian called by God. But his illness was a blessing in that it gave him a reprieve from the intensity of his daily workload. To his surprise, other desires then surfaced—including desires to find a partner, to work in other cultural settings, to attend seminary, and to reflect on his ten years of work as a Christian in the justice system.

Clark began to face the fact of his dissatisfaction with the work he thought God had called him to, and his fear of walking away from it. This led him to explore a long-denied interest in journalism, documentary films, and teaching overseas. Within two years, he found himself back to full strength, married, and encouraged by his wife to enroll at a seminary where his study of Scripture sharpened his skills of narrative, bringing out the true depth of a story. Today, it enables him to make documentary films with an understanding of religious history and theology that few in his industry have. And he also gets to teach college students.

Clark now says that for this period of his life, his heart's desires have been more than honored by God, but he wonders what new adventures he might be called to since he now sees a pattern in God's guidance. It was only through facing the unknown depths of his desires that he found the freedom to fulfill any of his ambitions: to assist young people, to marry, to travel widely, and to write and make films that promote the reality of God's reconciling grace at work in the secular world. He thinks there is more to discover about what he's made for by trusting that God is indeed guiding his steps.

 *Food for Thought*

What would you say was the crux of the problem for Clark in the story above? What dissatisfactions and desires do you shrug off in the daily grind of your working life? Could they be clues about a deeper, God-given desire?

_____

_____

_____

_____

_____

_____

It can be exceedingly difficult to get in touch with our deepest desires. Our motivations can become so confused by the sin and the brokenness of the world that our immediate or apparent desires blanket our hearts like a fog, obscuring the true desire that God has implanted in our inmost being.

> Sin, seizing an opportunity in the commandment, produced in me all kinds of covetousness. Apart from the law sin lies dead. . . . I do not understand my own actions. For I do not do what I want, but I do the very thing I hate. . . . So I find it to be a law that when I want to do what is good, evil lies close at hand. For I delight in the law of God in my inmost self, but I see in my members another law at war with the law of my mind, making me captive to the law of sin that dwells in my members. (Rom. 7:8, 15, 21–23)

For this reason, one cannot just say, "Do what makes you happy." What makes you happy—or seems to make you happy—might arise from distorted or sinful impulses. Or to put it another way, the things that appeal to you on the surface might be be far from meeting the needs of the world, using your skills and gifts for good, or even from fulfilling your authentic desires. The opposite is often true as well. The work that would fulfill your true desires appears at first to be undesirable, perhaps unreachable, so it may require great sacrifice and difficult labor. It's also possible that your truest desires might be met in many areas of your life, not necessarily solely in work.

Knowing what you sincerely desire requires spiritual maturity—perhaps more than you may have at the moment when you're facing a decision. But you can at least get rid of the idea that God will call you to something you hate. Capturing the heart of the matter, Frederick Buechner writes, "The place God calls you to is where your deep gladness and the world's deep hunger meet."

 Food for Thought

What do you think are your deepest desires? Think about them and what they may indicate about: How you spend your free time; what you spend your money on; how you organize your life; what you are anxious about not acquiring. If any these aren't following your true God-given desires, what can you do to get back on track?

_____

_____

_____

_____

_____

_____

Prayer

Pause for a few moments of silence to reflect on this lesson. Then offer a prayer, either spontaneous or by using the following:

Lord,

Thank you for the true, deepest desires you have implanted in us. Forgive us for letting them become buried, obscured, or twisted by the wrong desires. Show us what you truly want for us, and release our true desires for you and your world.

Amen.

Chapter 4

Further Discernment of God's Guidance to a Particular Kind of Work

Lesson #1: Freedom in Christ (Galatians 5:13–15, 22–26)

While these three considerations—the needs of the world, your skills and gifts, and your truest desires—are guides, they are not absolutes. You can't simply plug them into a formula to compute your calling. In a fallen world, you may have very little ability to choose your job anyway. In fact, most people have had jobs they didn't like, and this continues today.

Throughout history, many have been slaves, farmers, or home-makers, which is still the case in much of the world. Undoubtedly, some have enjoyed doing these tasks, but many have longed to do something else—surely no one ever wanted to be a slave.

The circumstances of this fallen world dictate that many toil in a profession they don't like. Yet under God's care, even a bad job can be a blessing (Jer. 37:7–9; 39:18). God is with you wherever you work. In many cases, it may be better to come to grips with the job you have—and find ways to participate in Christ's mission through it—than to try to find a job you think you'll like better.

 *Food for Thought*

Do you feel called to your present job? Why or why not? What can you do in your current employment to participate in Christ's work of creation, sustenance, and reconciliation?

_____

_____

_____

_____

_____

_____

_____

Freedom and Calling

Even in developed economies, many have little choice about the kind of work they do for a living. The Christian community would do well to equip us to make choices about our profession and to cope with and follow God's leading in whatever work we find ourselves doing.

Whatever your job, God's gifts enable you to labor for the common good, to find more contentment in your occupation, and to overcome or endure the negative aspects of your situation. Most importantly, God promises eventual liberation from work's toil, sweaty labor, and thistles.

Even if you do have the freedom to choose your job, the three issues we have been considering—the needs of the world, your gifts and skills, and your truest desires—are guides, not dictators. In Christ, believers have perfect freedom:

"So if the Son makes you free, you will be free indeed." (John 8:36)

> Now the Lord is the Spirit, and where the Spirit of the Lord is, there is freedom. (2 Cor. 3:17)

That means you have the freedom to take risks, make mistakes, and fail. God might lead you to a job you know nothing about, have no present knack for, and don't think you'd like. Would you be willing to take that job?

Conversely, you might conclude late in life that you missed God's professional calling for you. Take heart, for at the end you will not be judged on having had the right job or "fulfilling your God-given potential." You will be judged on the merits of Jesus Christ, applied to you only by God's grace in giving you faith. The calling to belong to Christ is God's only indispensable calling.

 Food for Thought

It seems we live between a broken reality and God's promise of total restoration of life as it was meant to be. How does this truth free you to be more accepting of your current work circumstances? What could change for you at work if you began living more deliberately within this sense of freedom in Christ?

_____

_____

_____

_____

_____

_____

_____

The body of Christ on earth is found in the community of believers (Rom. 12:5). Therefore, an experience of freedom in Christ and the discovery of God's calling are best ascertained in dialogue with the community, not in isolation.

We have already seen that the needs of the world (a form of community) are important as you discern *what* kind of work God is leading you toward. The community is also an important factor in *how* you discern God's leading. What do others perceive as God's leading for you? What gifts and skills and deepest desires do they see in you? Engage in discussions about God's calling with those who know you well. It may be wise to talk with a spiritual companion or mentor, to gather feedback from people you work closely with, or to ask a group of people to meet with you regularly as you discern God's leading for you.

Community is also an essential element in determining *who* is led to the different kinds of work needed in the world. Many people may have similar gifts and desires that can help meet the needs of the world, but it may not be that God wants *all* of them to do the same work. You need to discern the work God is not only leading you to, but also the work he is leading others to.

The community needs a balanced ensemble of workers working in harmony. For example, physicians bring powerful gifts and skills—and frequently a deep desire for healing—to help meet the world's great needs for physical mending. Yet, in the United States at least, there may be too many specialists and a deficiency in primary care physicians. One by one, medical students are matching their gifts, desires, and the needs of the world to discern a leading toward medicine. But overall, the ensemble of physicians is out of balance. Students need to have greater coordination as they select their courses of study, and patient care centers should know the needed mix of doctors. Discerning God's calling is a community endeavor.

Food for Thought

In what ways did you exercise individual choice regarding your current occupation? In what ways did other people or the community give you input? Do you think there was the optimum balance of individual choice and community input? If not, why?

_____

_____

_____

_____

_____

_____

_____

_____

Prayer

Pause for a few moments of silence to reflect on this lesson. Then offer a prayer, either spontaneous or by using the following:

Lord,

Help us to look beyond our individual occupational choices and to seek input from others. Bring us into faithful communities who know us and our intended vocations well enough to give us trustworthy help in discerning your call.

Amen.

Lesson #2: Church Work—A Higher Calling? (2 Timothy 2:15–25)

Many Christians have the impression that church workers—evangelists, missionaries, pastors, priests, ministers, and the like—have a higher calling than other workers. While there is little in the Bible to support this impression, by the Middle Ages "religious" life—in those days, life as a monastic—was widely considered holier than ordinary life. Regrettably, this distortion remains influential in churches of all traditions, even though the doctrine of virtually every church today affirms the equal value of the work of laypeople. In the Bible, God calls people to both church-related and nonchurch-related work. Let us look at some examples.

Calls to Church Work

"Then bring near to you your brother Aaron, and his sons with him, from among the Israelites, to serve me as priests—Aaron and Aaron's sons, Nadab and Abihu, Eleazar and Ithamar." (Exod. 28:1)

As Jesus passed along the Sea of Galilee, he saw Simon and his brother Andrew casting a net into the sea—for they were fishermen. And Jesus said to them, "Follow me and I will make you fish for people." (Mark 1:16–17)

While they were worshiping the Lord and fasting, the Holy Spirit said, "Set apart for me Barnabas and Saul for the work to which I have called them." . . . When they arrived at Salamis, they proclaimed the word of God in the synagogues of the Jews. And they had John also to assist them. (Acts 13:2, 5)

As we have already seen (chapter 2, lesson #3), direct, unmistakable calls such as these are highly unusual. In these particular cases, they were calls to priestly and missionary work. God does indeed call some people to work full time in pastoral, evangelistic, and other church-related professions.

 *Food for Thought*

Why do you think that so many people have the impression that a calling from God always—or usually—means a calling to become a pastor, missionary, or other religious worker? How have you been affected by this tendency?

_____

_____

_____

_____

_____

_____

_____

_____

Calls to Nonchurch Work

The Bible also depicts God's call to some people to work in secular occupations.

> The LORD said to Moses, "Your time to die is near; call Joshua and present yourselves in the tent of meeting, so that I may commission him." (Deut. 31:14)

> [David] was ruddy, and had beautiful eyes, and was handsome. The LORD said, "Rise and anoint him; for this is the one." Then Samuel took the horn of oil, and anointed him in the presence of his brothers; and the spirit of the LORD came mightily upon David from that day forward. Samuel then set out and went to Ramah. (1 Sam. 16:12–13)

It is worth noting that Moses and Joshua were both primarily military/political leaders, not cultic/religious leaders. They both had exceptional access to converse with God, but that doesn't make them religious leaders. Rather, it shows that God guides people in various walks of life, as he wants and whenever he chooses.

David was called as a military leader/protector and king of his people. So as we read the earliest books of Scripture, we see that it is inaccurate to think that God calls only church workers directly, unmistakably, and personally. This applies to *all* workers and professions.

Some confusion may arise in making sense of the difference between direct, unmistakable, and personal calls and the more subtle guidance that God typically provides. The confusion is often because many churches require that their pastors, priests, or other ministers be "called" to be ordained or to serve. Often, the word *call* is used to describe the process of selecting a minister or the decision to enter church work full time. However—unlike the examples of Aaron, Simon and Andrew, Saul and Barnabas, Moses, Joshua, and David—these situations are rarely direct, unmistakable, personal calls from God. Rather, candidates for church ministry would mostly describe their sense of "call" as a strong sense of guidance by God over time. This is more the normal way God calls people into specific forms of work.

 Food for Thought

What is the difference between receiving a direct, unmistakable, personal call from God and a less dramatic, long-term sense of God's guidance? How has this clarified or perhaps caused you to revise your own sense of being called to your particular work?

_____

_____

\
\
\
\
\

Prayer

Pause for a few moments of silence to reflect on this lesson. Then offer a prayer, either spontaneous or by using the following:

Lord,

We acknowledge that there is dignity in all forms of legitimate work. Help us to recognize your calls and to encourage all laborers to serve you faithfully in every occupation.

Amen.

Lesson #3: All Work Is Subject to God's Calling (Romans 12:2–21)

As we have seen, God's guidance can occur just as strongly in nonchurch-related professions as in church jobs. Church work is not in general a higher calling, and the term "call" applies just as much to nonchurch work as to church work.

We also affirm that nonchurch work is as much "full-time Christian service" as church work. All Christians are commanded to conduct everything they do as full-time service to Christ: "Whatever your task, put yourselves into it, as done for the Lord and not for your masters" (Col. 3:23).

Food for Thought

Knowing that God calls people into both church and nonchurch work, how does this affect your vocation? How would it benefit your Christian community to accept this conclusion, if they haven't considered it? If your community already lives in this realization, how does that play out in your working lives?

_____

_____

_____

_____

_____

_____

_____

There is one stream of thought that views the following Scripture as contradicting the view we have just laid out:

> Let the elders who rule well be considered worthy of double honor, especially those who labor in preaching and teaching; for the scripture says, "You shall not muzzle an ox while it is treading out the grain," and, "The laborer deserves to be paid." (1 Tim. 5:17–18)

According to this perspective, being a pastor and teacher is a "double honor" compared to other professions. But most Bible commentaries reject this interpretation. The passage's true comparison is among pastors, not between pastors and laypeople. Alternately, the contrast may be between elders who volunteer in their spare time and elders who work full time for the church. So a careful reading suggests that elders who do their work well are worthy of a double honor (or honorarium), compared to elders who do their work merely adequately.

The Old Testament quotations about wages further reinforce the sense that this passage is about rewarding high-performing or full-time elders, not about comparing church work to other work. It means that elders who work skillfully and diligently deserve to be paid well by the church.

 Food for Thought

Why do you think this "double honor" in 1 Timothy has been interpreted by some to mean that a pastor's job is of a higher order than any other work?

_____

_____

_____

_____

_____

The only jobs that do not have equal status in God's eyes are those that require work forbidden by the Bible or that are incompatible with its values. For example, jobs requiring murder, adultery, stealing, false witness, or greed (Exod. 20:13–17), usury (Lev. 25:26), damage to health (Matt. 10:8), or harm to the environment (Gen. 2:15) are immoral in God's sight.

This is not to say that *people* who do these jobs have lesser status in God's eyes. People whose circumstances lead them to illicit work are not necessarily worse than other people. For example, although Deuteronomy 22:21 condemns prostitution, Christ's response to prostitutes was not condemnation but deliverance (Luke 7:47–50; Matt. 21:31–32). Jobs of this sort might be the lesser of two evils in certain situations, but they are never God's desired work for someone.

Food for Thought

How do you distinguish between sinful jobs (such as prostitution) and the people employed in them? What are some ways we could follow Jesus in delivering people from illegal occupations into legal ones?

_____

_____

_____

_____

_____

_____

_____

_____

Prayer

Pause for a few moments of silence to reflect on this lesson. Then offer a prayer, either spontaneous or by using the following:

Lord,

It is so freeing when the church regards all work as important to you, not just church work. Help us to encourage your people to follow your divine call, and help us also to be willing to help those trapped in destructive work to find their call in a dignified occupation.

Amen.

Chapter 5

Discerning Whether to Change Jobs

Lesson #1: Two Scenarios (1 Corinthians 7:17–24; Matthew 25:14–23)

Since God leads his people to their work, could it ever be acceptable to change jobs? Wouldn't that be rejecting God's guidance to the career you already have?

Martin Luther, the sixteenth-century Protestant theologian, famously argued against changing jobs. This was based largely on his understanding of 1 Corinthians 7:20: "Let each of you remain in the condition in which you were called." Luther equated "condition" with occupation and concluded that it was not legitimate for Christians to change positions.

However, Luther's contemporary John Calvin did not accept this interpretation—and most modern theologians do not either. For one thing, it doesn't seem to take sufficient account of the next verse, which suggests that changing jobs is allowed, at least in some circumstances: "Were you a slave when called? Do not be concerned about it. Even if you can gain your freedom, make use of your present condition now more than ever" (1 Cor. 7:21).

 *Food for Thought*

What are some reasons people might stay in careers for the long haul, and what are some reasons why people switch from job to job? Which of these ideas relates to the three factors we discussed as God's guidance for our work? How does that answer whether or not we should change jobs?

_____

_____

_____

_____

_____

_____

_____

Miroslav Volf says that since the factors by which God guides people to work may change over the course of a working life, God may indeed lead people to change their profession. The needs of the world may change. Our gifts and skills may increase (or diminish). Our desires may alter. As our capabilities grow with our experience in serving God, he may lead us to bigger tasks with more responsibilities that require us to change jobs. "Well done, good and trustworthy slave; you have been trustworthy in a few things, I will put you in charge of many things; enter into the joy of your master" (Matt. 25:21).

Conversely, if you become a Christian later in life, you might ask yourself if God *requires* you to change jobs. It might seem that finding new life in Christ means acquiring a new job or career. Generally, however, this is not the case.

Since there is no hierarchy of professions, it is usually a mistake to think God wants you to find a "higher calling" upon becoming a Christian. Unless your job is immoral, or your industry or colleagues threaten to keep you stuck in sinful habits, there may be no need to change jobs.

Whether you switch occupations or not, you probably sense the need to do your work *differently* because you are a Christian, paying attention to biblical commands, values, and virtues. This is what happened to Zacchaeus the tax collector.

> When Jesus came to the place, he looked up and said to him, "Zacchaeus, hurry and come down; for I must stay at your house today." So he hurried down and was happy to welcome him. All who saw it began to grumble and said, "He has gone to be the guest of one who is a sinner." Zacchaeus stood there and said to the Lord, "Look, half of my possessions, Lord, I will give to the poor; and if I have defrauded anyone of anything, I will pay back four times as much." Then Jesus said to him, "Today salvation has come to this house, because he too is a son of Abraham." (Luke 19:5–9)

 Food for Thought

Have you ever wanted to change your profession? Have you ever thought that God wanted you to switch jobs? How did you handle such situations? Would you look it at them the same way now?

_____

_____

_____

_____

_____

_____

Prayer

Pause for a few moments of silence to reflect on this lesson. Then offer a prayer, either spontaneous or by using the following:

Lord,

We thank you for the gift of work. Please give us the opportunity to follow your guidance to a career, and the faithfulness to fulfill our tasks worthily even when we would prefer not to. Guide us when we are offered the opportunity for a new job or career.

Amen.

Lesson #2: Discerning God's Guidance into a Particular Job— Case Study #1 (Genesis 39:1–6; 41:37–45)

Almost forty years ago, a South Asian widower of the lowest social class, who had six children to care for, decided it was time for the eldest child, Mara, to join him as a coolie (a low-paid, unskilled worker) in the fields of a local farm owner. His daughter could help with providing income to support the household. He was not only a social outcast, but as a Christian he was also a religious outcast.

A father and daughter took the bus each morning from outside their village to the hills where they manually cultivated and harvested rice for the landowner. Every day at the bus stop, the father pointed out to Mara a school teacher who rode by on a bicycle in his suit and tie: "You could be like that school teacher." Over the next year he added, "When you become a teacher, teach something you are particularly interested in, not just the general things others might teach."

When Mara was twelve, her father took her to a Christian missionary orphanage and left her there. He knew the missionaries would provide her with the education she needed. Mara never lived in her father's home again.

 Food for Thought

This story is an example of caste groups locked into servitude for generations. The need for children to go to work in order to support the family seemingly cuts off any educational opportunities that could have led to the escape from the cycle of poverty. How would you feel if you were in this situation? Where is the call of God in this story so far?

_____

_____

_____

_____

_____

_____

Mara excelled at high school and graduated with a scholarship to attend a major South Asian university. She had been profoundly influenced by the generosity and encouragement of the missionaries to pursue her father's dream of her becoming a teacher. It was during those high school years that Mara gave her allegiance to Christ.

At university, Mara excelled again, specializing in the history of her country and the impact of European colonization, eventually earning a doctorate. Winning scholarships to undertake further research in her field, she traveled to European universities to study in their archives and libraries. Over the course of sixteen years, she earned three more doctorates, including one specializing in education.

For the next twenty-five years, Mara found opportunities to teach in top U.S. and U.K. universities in endowed chairs, becoming an expert on the impact of colonization in South Asia. With those opportunities has come an ongoing freedom to travel back to her homeland, bringing Western graduate students to learn the realities of life there at a grass-roots level and to teach the underserved students of lower castes in her homeland.

Mara was also able to provide income for her elderly father and younger family members, and she was able to see him finish life with a sense of fulfillment as a coolie working in the service of God.

 Food for Thought

The father and daughter in our study could never have imagined the trajectory of her life when she was first dropped off at the orphanage by her father. How do you see a call of God playing out in her circumstances? What would it mean to you to have to choose between leaving your family's home at a young age to pursue education and staying at home with no opportunity to escape a life of poverty?

_____

_____

_____

_____

_____

_____

While this may sound like a fairy tale, it isn't. All along the way, Mara had to deal with religious and ideological marginalization, both at home and in Western academia. It has been a journey of utmost challenge to her character. Prejudice regarding her dark skin continues to dog her steps at the highest levels of Western academy and broader white society, despite her earned credentials. And caste-based prejudice in her homeland remains a permanent point of resistance to her scholarship there. Yet to this day, she continues to influence the scholarship of her field from a senior professorial position in a Western university. She also finds fulfillment in her work as a wife and mother.

She still maintains her focus on the call of the God who rescued her from servitude. Only through doing this, she says, can she continue to avoid the jealousy, anger, and bitterness that would compromise her enjoyment of her work. If she gave in to those feelings, they might diminish her gratefulness to her biological father whose love of Christ made it possible for her to become a teacher in the first place.

 Food for Thought

Given Mara's obstacles, are you surprised at her achievements? How important do you think her calling must have been in order for her to deal with obstacles (and, as she admits, in an imperfect manner)? How can you apply that to your own circumstances?

_____

_____

_____

_____

_____

Prayer

Pause for a few moments of silence to reflect on this lesson. Then offer a prayer, either spontaneous or by using the following:

Lord,

How wonderfully you work in the lives of devoted servants to bring blessing not only to their own lives but also to generations to come. Help us to view our circumstances in light of Mara's story and the hope of blessing so clearly illustrated by this father and daughter. Help us to look up from our own forms of bondage and discover your call for our lives.

Amen.

Chapter 6

Conclusions about Calling

Lesson #1: Discerning God's Guidance into a Particular Job— Case Study #2 (Psalm 37:1–9, 23–27; Ephesians 5:22–33)

By the time he completed high school, Sam was pretty sure he wanted to build houses. He had some experience in school where he excelled at leading others in home construction on missions trips to South America. He saw this as part of the way God had equipped him for whatever work lay ahead, feeling that nonprofit work was the direction he should go. So Sam went on to be trained in home construction through a community college in Illinois.

Having done well on job sites, he was surprised that his first real job opportunity, working with a for-profit construction company, was highly lucrative. The company was innovative in creating smaller-scale, affordable housing for underserved communities that were either too poor or too remote for most home building companies. Sam had just married and his first child was on the way, so he decided that taking the job was the right move.

 Food for Thought

Without reading ahead, what do you think was right about his decision? What would you have done if you were in a similar circumstance? Do you see any red flags so far?

_____

_____

_____

_____

_____

_____

_____

The job proved to be so challenging and the founder/CEO so driven that Sam found himself working seventy to eighty hours a week, away from home for up to three weeks at a time, for more than five years. He was trying to keep pace with growth that felt like a runaway horse. The carrot offered to him as compensation for the sacrificial effort was company stock options that would be realized when the business eventually sold out to a larger company.

Sam was certain that all in all this position was God's calling and chose to hang on, ignoring the cries of pain from his lonely wife until it was too late. She returned home to her parents with their two children to try and get his attention. Sam was also missing from his Christian community. His work had become all-consuming, and his justification became that most people just didn't understand the demands put on a Christian working for the common good at this level of business. In these ways he rationalized his isolation.

Although he began to wonder if he had missed something in his calling, Sam delayed responding to his wife. Then divorce papers arrived and the role of husband was taken from him. It was the pain of divorce that made him reevaluate the trajectory of his life.

He still had a legal responsibility for his children, and so began his search for a job that would give him hours to spend with them and money to provide for their welfare.

 *Food for Thought*

Name the red flags that appeared as his career took shape in this innovative company. How should he have responded, and what do you think was God's real call in the situation? What do you imagine obscured his ability to hear this call?

_____

_____

_____

_____

_____

_____

_____

Sam found a church community with many younger business-people like himself, where the traps he had fallen into were well known. Participating in classes that dealt with faith in the workplace, he found the courage to take a job as a builder with a much-reduced salary for a nonprofit organization, renovating housing for inner-city poor. He rediscovered his past skills and how much he enjoyed his work. A further blessing that came as a result was the time he now had to spend with his children.

Eventually, he rose to be vice president in the organization. Ten years after his divorce, he married a divorced woman who was able to identify with his journey. But the challenges were not over.

During a time of transition to a new CEO, the outgoing CEO came under pressure from the board of directors to retire Sam from the organization. Sam thought that the CEO was a friend, until the day the CEO called him into his office.

That encounter was as painful as his divorce. The CEO exploded angrily that Sam was completely unfit, unskilled, and without any discernible gift for administering building and renovation. The CEO said that Sam was in the wrong job altogether. He demanded that Sam resign or face being sacked. To Sam's surprise, tears streamed down his face as he left that office.

Through the counsel of his wife and church confidants, he maintained his sense of dignity and the certainty of his call, and sent in his letter of resignation without expressing any anger or bitterness at the injustice he had just experienced.

Within two months, a much larger housing organization heard of his availability and sought to employ him. He took a position as vice president of Inner City Projects, and within a year he assembled funding and a team of extraordinary professional builders, shepherding them through an early completion of the largest project ever undertaken in the organization's history. He continues to be a loving husband and now a grandfather. Keeping one eye on the weather at board level, Sam remains happily serving the organization that truly recognized his gifts.

 Food for Thought

Faithfulness doesn't necessarily shield us from injustice and violence in the workplace. What surprises you about Sam's journey? How would you expect a person in his position to respond to such a blindside attack on his competence and his sense of calling? Have you ever found yourself in a similar situation? If so, what was your reaction?

_____

_____

_____

_____

_____

Prayer

Pause for a few moments of silence to reflect on this lesson. Then offer a prayer, either spontaneous or by using the following:

Lord,

You never said it would be easy to serve you in our occupations or that circumstances would never call us to question our calling. But we thank you for how you continually prove that you never turn your back on your children. Thank you for turning Sam's life around and for using his story as a lesson about your graciousness. Help us to be gracious when we have to accept some bitter defeats. We hope in you alone, since you said that the promise of blessing for faithful obedience is not only for this life, but also for the life to come.

Amen.

Lesson #2: Concluding Reflections (Psalm 111)

We have discovered that how we work is as important to God as what jobs or professions we have. In every job, we have the opportunities to meet people's needs, to employ our gifts and skills, and to express—or discover—our deepest desires. Our decisions to serve God *today* are more important than positioning ourselves for our imagined "right jobs" tomorrow. In fact, the little we may be able to do in God's service today is often the key to being able to do more in the future. Jesus said, "Whoever is faithful in a very little is faithful also in much" (Luke 16:10).

We must take seriously God's call to us to various kinds of ordinary work. In doing so, we are correcting the longstanding tendency of many Christians to regard ordinary work as unimportant to God and unworthy of his calling. In the same way, it would be equally wrong to elevate the importance of our professions to idolatry. Getting the right job does not bring salvation or even happiness. Moreover, the true aim of work for Christians is to serve the common good, not to advance our own interests. Over a lifetime, serving the common good comes far more from doing each day's work to the best of our ability in Christ, than it does from finding the best occupation for ourselves.

 Food for Thought

What have you learned or thought most deeply about during the course of this study? Has your understanding of God's calling to work changed? Have any questions been raised that you would like to pursue further? What is your sense of God's calling to you in your career?

_____

_____

_____

_____

_____

_____

_____

_____

Wisdom for Using This Study in the Workplace

Community within the workplace is a good thing, and a Christian community within the workplace is even better. Sensitivity is needed, however, when we get together in the workplace (even a Christian workplace) to enjoy fellowship time together, learn what the Bible has to say about our work, and encourage one another in Jesus' name. When you meet at your place of employment, here are some guidelines to keep in mind:

- Be sensitive to your surroundings. Know your company policy about having such a group on company property. Make sure not to give the impression that this is a secret or exclusive group.

- Be sensitive to time constraints. Don't go over your allotted time. Don't be late to work! Make sure you are a good witness to the others (especially non-Christians) in your workplace by being fully committed to your work during working hours and doing all your work with excellence.

- Be sensitive to the shy or silent members of your group. Encourage everyone in the group and give them a chance to talk.

- Be sensitive to the others by being prepared. Read the Bible study material and Scripture passages and think about your answers to the questions ahead of time.

These Bible studies are based on the Theology of Work biblical commentary. Besides reading the commentary, please visit the Theology of Work website (www.theologyofwork.org) for videos, interviews, and other material on the Bible and your work.

Leader's Guide

Living Word. It is always exciting to start a new group and study. The possibilities of growth and relationship are limitless when we engage with one another and with God's word. Always remember that God's word is "alive and active, sharper than any double-edged sword" (Heb. 4:12) and when you study his word, it should change you.

A Way Has Been Made. Please know you and each person joining your study have been prayed for by people you will probably never meet who share your faith. And remember that "the LORD himself goes before you and will be with you; he will never leave you nor forsake you. Do not be afraid; do not be discouraged" (Deut. 31:8). As a leader, you need to know that truth. Remind yourself of it throughout this study.

Pray. It is always a good idea to pray for your study and those involved weeks before you even begin. It is recommended to pray for yourself as leader, your group members, and the time you are about to spend together. It's no small thing you are about to start and the more you prepare in the Spirit, the better. Apart from Jesus, we can do nothing (John 14:5). Remain in him and "you will bear much fruit" (John 15:5). It's also a good idea to have trusted friends pray and intercede for you and your group as you work through the study.

Spiritual Battle. Like it or not, the Bible teaches that we are in the middle of a spiritual battle. The enemy would like nothing more than for this study to be ineffective. It would be part of his scheme to have group members not show up or engage in any discussion. His victory would be that your group just passes time together going through the motions of a yet another Bible study. You, as a leader, are a threat to the enemy, as it is your desire to lead people down the path of righteousness (as taught in Proverbs). Read Ephesians 6:10–20 and put your armor on.

Scripture. Prepare before your study by reading the selected Scripture verses ahead of time.

Chapters. Each chapter contains approximately three lessons. As you work through the lessons, keep in mind the particular chapter theme in connection with the lessons. These lessons are designed so that you can go through them in thirty minutes each.

Lessons. Each lesson has teaching points with their own discussion questions. This format should keep the participants engaged with the text and one another.

Food for Thought. The questions at the end of the teaching points are there to create discussion and deepen the connection between each person and the content being addressed. You know the people in your group and should feel free to come up with your own questions or adapt the ones provided to best meet the needs of your group. Again, this would require some preparation beforehand.

Opening and Closing Prayers. Sometimes prayer prompts are given before and usually after each lesson. These are just suggestions. You know your group and the needs present, so please feel free to pray accordingly.

Bible Commentary. The Theology of Work series contains a variety of books to help you apply the Scriptures and Christian faith to your work. This Bible study is based on the *Theology of Work Bible Commentary*, examining what the Bible say about work. This commentary is intended to assist those with theological training or interest to conduct in-depth research into passages or books of Scripture.

Video Clips. The Theology of Work website (www.theologyofwork .org) provides good video footage of people from the marketplace highlighting the teaching from all the books of the Bible. It would be great to incorporate some of these videos into your teaching time.

Enjoy your study! Remember that God's word does not return void—ever. It produces fruit and succeeds in whatever way God has intended it to succeed.

> "So shall my word be that goes out from my mouth;
>   it shall not return to me empty,
>   but it shall accomplish that which I purpose,
>   and succeed in the thing for which I sent it." (Isa. 55:11)

"This commentary was written exactly for those of us who aim to integrate our faith and work on a daily basis and is an excellent reminder that God hasn't called the world to go to the church, but has called the Church to go to the world."

BONNIE WURZBACHER

FORMER SENIOR VICE PRESIDENT, THE COCA-COLA COMPANY

HENDRICKSON PUBLISHERS   THEOLOGY OF WORK   PROJECT

Explore what the Bible has to say about work, book by book.

THE BIBLE AND YOUR WORK
Study Series